T Gomathi
L Megalan Leo
A Aranganathan

PIEZOELECTRIC ENERGY HARVESTER

T Gomathi
L Megalan Leo
A Aranganathan

PIEZOELECTRIC ENERGY HARVESTER

MEMS OPTICAL SWITCH FOR PIEZOELECTRIC ENERGY HARVESTER

LAP LAMBERT Academic Publishing

Imprint

Cover image: www.ingimage.com

Publisher:
LAP LAMBERT Academic Publishing
is a trademark of
Dodo Books Indian Ocean Ltd. and OmniScriptum S.R.L publishing group

120 High Road, East Finchley, London, N2 9ED, United Kingdom
Str. Armeneasca 28/1, office 1, Chisinau MD-2012, Republic of Moldova, Europe
Managing Directors: Ieva Konstantinova, Victoria Ursu
info@omniscriptum.com

Printed at: see last page
ISBN: 978-620-8-49549-7

MEMS OPTICAL SWITCH FOR PIEZOELECTRIC ENERGY HARVESTER

Abstract

The work presents the design and implementation of a micro-electromechanical system (MEMS) optical switch integrated with a piezoelectric energy harvester. The proposed device addresses the growing demand for sustainable and autonomous micro/nanosystems by harnessing ambient mechanical vibrations to generate electrical energy, thereby eliminating the need for external power sources.The core component of the system is a piezoelectric cantilever beam that converts mechanical vibrations into electrical energy through the direct piezoelectric effect. This harvested energy is utilized to actuate the MEMS optical switch, enabling its operation without external power. The integration of energy harvesting and switching functions into a single MEMS device not only reduces the overall system size but also enhances its reliability and efficiency.The design process involved optimizing the cantilever beam's dimensions and material properties to maximize energy conversion efficiency while ensuring sufficient mechanical displacement for effective optical switching. Advanced microfabrication techniques were employed to realize the device, and comprehensive simulations were conducted to predict its performance under various vibration conditions. Experimental validation confirmed the device's capability to operate the optical switch using energy harvested from ambient vibrations, demonstrating its potential for applications in remote sensing, optical communication, and other fields requiring self-powered microscale devices.This work contributes to the advancement of self-sustaining MEMS technologies by demonstrating the feasibility of integrating energy harvesting and functional components into a compact, efficient, and autonomous system.

TABLE OF CONTENT

LIST OF FIGURES

CHAPTER 1

INTRODUCTION

The rapid advancement of optical communication systems has led to an increasing demand for efficient, compact, and low-power optical switching technologies. MicroElectro-Mechanical Systems (MEMS) optical switches have emerged as a promising solution, offering high-speed operation, low insertion loss, and scalability for dense photonic integration. MEMS-based optical switches utilize microfabricated movable components, such as mirrors or waveguides, to control optical signal paths. These switches are crucial in applications ranging from optical fiber networks to aerospace and biomedical sensing. However, traditional MEMS optical switches often rely on external power sources, which can limit their deployment in remote or energy-constrained environments. To overcome this limitation, integrating MEMS optical switches with piezoelectric energy harvesters presents an innovative approach to developing self-powered optical switching systems.

Piezoelectric energy harvesting is a technique that converts mechanical vibrations into electrical energy using piezoelectric materials. These materials generate electrical charge in response to mechanical stress, enabling energy capture from ambient vibrations, acoustic waves, or mechanical motion. This self-sustaining power generation method is particularly advantageous for MEMS devices, as it reduces dependence on external power supplies and enhances system reliability. In the context of MEMS optical switches, piezoelectric energy harvesters can provide the necessary power to actuate the switch, making them ideal for applications in remote sensing, autonomous systems, and next-generation optical networks.

1.1 Significance of MEMS Optical Switches

MEMS optical switches offer several advantages over traditional optical switching technologies, such as mechanical relays and liquid crystal switches. Their small form factor, fast response times, and low power consumption make them highly suitable for modern optical communication networks. Conventional optical switches often require bulky electro-mechanical components or active electronic circuits, leading to higher power consumption and increased maintenance requirements.

MEMS optical switches, on the other hand, leverage microfabrication techniques to achieve precise control of optical signals with minimal energy expenditure.

One of the primary mechanisms employed in MEMS optical switches is the use of micro-mirrors or micro-cantilevers to redirect light paths. These components can be electrostatically or mechanically actuated to achieve switching functions. Electrostatic actuation, while widely used, typically requires an external voltage source. In contrast, a piezoelectric-based actuation mechanism can enable selfpowered operation by harvesting ambient mechanical energy. This advancement is particularly crucial for applications in space missions, remote fiber optic networks, and autonomous sensor systems where power availability is a limiting factor.

1.2 Piezoelectric Energy Harvesting for MEMS Optical Switches

Piezoelectric energy harvesting has gained significant attention in recent years due to its ability to convert mechanical vibrations into usable electrical energy. Piezoelectric materials such as lead zirconate titanate (PZT), aluminum nitride (AlN), and zinc oxide (ZnO) have demonstrated high energy conversion efficiency and durability, making them suitable for MEMS applications. When integrated with a MEMS optical switch, a piezoelectric harvester can eliminate the need for external power sources by generating electricity from environmental vibrations or mechanical motion.

The working principle of a piezoelectric energy harvester involves the deformation of the piezoelectric material under an applied force or vibration. This deformation generates a charge across the material's surface, which can be stored in capacitors or used directly to power a micro-actuator. For MEMS optical switches, this energy can be utilized to move micro-mirrors, align optical waveguides, or modulate optical signals without requiring an external power source. The integration of such a system not only enhances energy efficiency but also improves device longevity and operational sustainability.

1.3 Challenges in Piezoelectric MEMS Optical Switch Integration

Despite the advantages of piezoelectric MEMS optical switches, several challenges must be addressed to achieve optimal performance. One of the key challenges is the efficiency of energy harvesting. Piezoelectric materials generate limited power output, which must be efficiently managed to ensure sufficient energy is available for switch actuation. The design of the piezoelectric harvester, including material selection, structural geometry, and vibration frequency optimization, plays a crucial role in maximizing energy output.

Another challenge is switching speed and reliability. MEMS optical switches require precise actuation to achieve accurate optical signal routing. Any delay or instability in the actuation mechanism could result in signal degradation or increased insertion loss. Ensuring the robustness of the piezoelectric actuator under varying environmental conditions, such as temperature fluctuations and mechanical stress, is essential for reliable long-term operation.

Additionally, fabrication complexity poses a challenge in integrating piezoelectric energy harvesters with MEMS optical switches. The microfabrication process must ensure compatibility between the piezoelectric material and the MEMS switch components. Deposition techniques, electrode patterning, and packaging must be carefully optimized to achieve high-performance integration without compromising device functionality.

1.4 Potential Applications of Self-Powered MEMS Optical Switches

The integration of piezoelectric energy harvesting with MEMS optical switches opens new opportunities for various applications. One of the most promising areas is optical fiber communication networks, where these switches can be used for dynamic wavelength routing, optical cross-connects, and network reconfiguration without the need for external power sources. This capability can significantly reduce energy consumption in large-scale optical networks and enhance their reliability.

In aerospace and satellite communication systems, self-powered MEMS optical switches can play a crucial role in optical signal modulation and beam steering.

Given the challenges of power availability in space, the ability to harvest energy from mechanical vibrations or structural movements can enable long-term, maintenancefree operation of optical components in satellite payloads.

Another key application is in biomedical sensing and wearable technology. MEMS optical switches can be integrated into bio-optical sensors for non-invasive monitoring of physiological parameters such as blood oxygen levels, glucose concentration, and neural activity. The self-powered nature of these devices ensures continuous operation without the need for battery replacements, making them ideal for long-term healthcare monitoring solutions.

1.5 Future Prospects and Research Directions

The future of MEMS optical switches with piezoelectric energy harvesting lies in optimizing energy conversion efficiency, reducing power losses, and improving actuation response time. Advanced materials, such as ferroelectric thin films and nanostructured piezoelectrics, offer promising solutions for enhancing energy harvesting capabilities. Moreover, integrating machine learning algorithms for adaptive energy management can enable real-time optimization of power usage based on environmental conditions.

Furthermore, research into hybrid energy harvesting systems, combining piezoelectric, photovoltaic, and thermoelectric methods, could further enhance the self-sustainability of MEMS optical switches. Such advancements will pave the way for next-generation intelligent photonic networks, autonomous sensor systems, and energy-efficient optical computing platforms.

1.5.1 Research Objective

- The objective of this research is to investigate and analyze the optical switching mechanism in microelectromechanical systems (MEMS)-based devices.
- The study explores the influence of electrical potential, displacement fields, and capacitance variations on the switching mechanism's performance.

* The research seeks to enhance the understanding of electro-optical interactions in MEMS structures by examining the relationship between applied voltage (V0) and key parameters such as displacement in the Z component and capacitance changes.
* The findings from this study will contribute to the development of efficient and reliable optical switching systems with potential applications in optical communication networks and photonic devices.

1.5.2 Research Hypothesis

Primary Hypothesis: Variations in applied voltage significantly influence the optical switching mechanism in MEMS-based devices, leading to measurable changes in displacement fields and capacitance.

1.5.2.1 Sub-Hypotheses:

- Increasing the applied voltage (V0) will result in a greater displacement in the Z component, affecting the structural deformation of the MEMS switch.
- The capacitance of the system will increase non-linearly with voltage due to the induced displacement and deformation of the switching elements. o The electric field distribution and mechanical displacement fields interact to modulate the optical switching behavior, which can be optimized for efficient signal transmission.

This hypothesis will be tested through computational modeling and experimental validation to understand the electro-optical interactions governing MEMS-based optical switches.

1.5.3 Research Contribution

The integration of MEMS (Micro-Electro-Mechanical Systems) optical switches with piezoelectric energy harvesters represents a novel approach to enhancing energy efficiency and enabling self-powered optoelectronic systems. This research contributes to the field in several key areas:

1.5.4 Design and Fabrication of MEMS Optical Switches

- Development of a miniaturized MEMS-based optical switch that operates using mechanical displacement controlled by piezoelectric actuation. o Use of microscale cantilevers or beams that deflect under mechanical stress, modulating optical signals for switching applications.
- Integration with silicon photonics or optical waveguides to enable precise optical signal control.

1.5.5 Piezoelectric Energy Harvesting for Self-Powered Operation

- Utilization of piezoelectric materials (e.g., PZT, AlN, ZnO) to convert ambient vibrations into electrical energy.
- Development of an energy-efficient switching mechanism that eliminates the need for external power sources.
- Optimization of the harvesting structure (cantilever, diaphragm, or bimorph designs) to maximize energy output.

Numerical simulation and experimental validation of displacement, stress distribution, and optical modulation efficiency.

Optimization of switching speed, insertion loss, and mechanical resonance to achieve high-performance switching.

Reduction of optical losses and mechanical damping for long-term reliability.

Applications in Low-Power Optical Communication and Sensing

Enabling self-powered optical communication systems, reducing reliance on batteries or wired power sources.

Potential applications in optical fiber networks, LiDAR systems, biomedical sensing, and smart optical grids.

Demonstration of a prototype MEMS optical switch driven by a piezoelectric harvester for real-world validation.

This research bridges the gap between MEMS optical switching and energy harvesting, contributing to developing autonomous, energy-efficient optoelectronic systems with potential applications in telecommunications, biomedical devices, and smart sensing networks.

1.6 Organization of the Research

Introduction: Discuss the proposed model's overall functionality and efficiency and its applications.

Literature Review – Study existing MEMS optical switches and piezoelectric energy harvesters to identify research gaps.

Conceptual Design – Develop a theoretical model for integrating a MEMS optical switch with a piezoelectric harvester.

Material Selection—For efficient performance, Choose suitable piezoelectric materials (e.g., PZT, AlN) and optical components.

Structural and Optical Simulation – Perform FEM simulations to analyze mechanical displacement, stress distribution, and optical signal modulation.

Fabrication Process – Manufacture the MEMS optical switch using microfabrication techniques (e.g., lithography, etching, deposition).

Experimental Testing – Measure mechanical deflection, energy harvesting efficiency, and optical switching performance.

Performance Optimization – Refine design parameters to enhance power output, optical efficiency, and switching speed.

Application Demonstration – Validate the prototype for real-world applications in optical communication or sensing systems.

CHAPTER 2

LITERATURE SURVEY

Hossain et al. (2023) provide a comprehensive review of MEMS-based energy harvesting devices designed for low-power applications, focusing on advancements in micro-electromechanical systems (MEMS) for efficient energy conversion. The study explores various energy harvesting mechanisms, including piezoelectric, electromagnetic, and electrostatic techniques, emphasizing their applications in wireless sensor networks, biomedical devices, and IoT systems. The authors discuss material selection, fabrication techniques, and performance optimization while highlighting the challenges of scalability, efficiency, and integration with electronic circuits. The review concludes by emphasizing the potential of hybrid energy harvesters and advanced nanomaterials to enhance energy output, ensuring sustainable power solutions for miniaturized electronic devices.

Muscalu et al. (2024) present a comprehensive study on piezoelectric MEMS energy harvesters designed for low-power applications. The research focuses on design optimization, material selection, and performance evaluation of MEMS-based energy harvesters that convert ambient vibrations into electrical power. The study highlights the use of lead zirconate titanate (PZT) and aluminum nitride (AlN) as piezoelectric materials, emphasizing their efficiency in low-frequency vibration environments. Experimental and simulation-based analyses demonstrate the harvester's ability to generate power in the microwatt to milliwatt range, making it suitable for applications in wireless sensor networks, IoT devices, and biomedical implants. The authors further discuss fabrication techniques, power conditioning circuits, and integration challenges, providing insights into future advancements in self-powered MEMS systems.

Mahmud et al. (2022) provide a comprehensive review of advancements in MEMS and microfluidics-based energy harvesting technologies, focusing on their efficiency, applications, and integration with modern systems. The study highlights piezoelectric, triboelectric, and electromagnetic micro-energy harvesters, emphasizing their role in self-powered sensors and biomedical devices. Notably, piezoelectric MEMS energy harvesters achieve power densities up to 100 μW/cm², while triboelectric nanogenerators (TENGs) reach efficiencies of over 50%. The review also discusses microfluidic approaches, where liquid-based energy harvesters generate power outputs exceeding 1 mW/cm² under optimized conditions. The authors conclude that MEMS-based harvesters have significant potential for wearable electronics, IoT devices, and implantable medical sensors, though challenges remain in scalability, energy storage integration, and long-term stability.

Ashford et al. (2021) investigated methods to enhance the output efficiency of a piezoelectric energy harvester using a synchronized switch harvesting on inductor (SSHI) design. Their study, presented at the 2021 IEEE Pulsed Power Conference, demonstrated that conventional energy harvesting circuits often suffer from low energy extraction efficiency due to phase mismatches and electrical damping losses. By implementing the SSHI technique, they achieved a 2.5× increase in power output compared to a standard rectifier-based energy harvester. The experimental setup utilized a PZT-based cantilever with a resonance frequency of 120 Hz, where the harvested power improved from 120 μW (standard circuit) to 300 μW (SSHI circuit) under the same excitation conditions. The study highlights that optimized switch timing and reduced voltage losses significantly contribute to higher power conversion efficiency, making SSHI a promising approach for self-powered microsystems and low-power electronics.

Brusa et al. (2023) conducted a comprehensive review on piezoelectric energy harvesting (PEH), focusing on materials, design strategies, and readout circuits. The study highlights that lead zirconate titanate (PZT) remains the most efficient piezoelectric material, with an energy conversion efficiency of up to 80%, while aluminum nitride (AlN) offers better CMOS compatibility despite lower efficiency (~50%). Various cantilever-based designs are analyzed, with optimal resonant frequencies ranging from 50 Hz to 1 kHz depending on application requirements. The study also reviews rectifier circuits, reporting that synchronized switch harvesting (SSH) techniques can enhance power output by 200–300% compared to traditional full-bridge rectifiers. Experimental results indicate that PEH systems can achieve power densities of 0.5–10 mW/cm², making them viable for wireless sensor networks, biomedical implants, and IoT applications. The review concludes that advancements in nanostructured piezoelectric films and hybrid energy harvesting systems will further improve efficiency and scalability.

Kumar et al. (2024) explore the applications of functionally graded (FG) nano- and microstructures in MEMS (Micro-Electro-Mechanical Systems) and NEMS (NanoElectro-Mechanical Systems), emphasizing their advantages in enhancing mechanical strength, thermal stability, and energy efficiency. The study discusses how gradual material property variations in FG structures improve stress distribution, reduce thermal mismatches, and enhance durability in MEMS/NEMS devices. Numerical results indicate that FG microcantilevers exhibit up to 30% lower stress concentrations compared to homogeneous structures, while FG nanosensors demonstrate a 20% improvement in sensitivity due to optimized material composition. Additionally, simulations reveal that FG resonators show a 15% increase in frequency stability, making them ideal for high-precision sensing and actuation applications. The study highlights the potential of FG nano/microstructures in piezoelectric energy harvesters, biomedical implants, and high-performance micro-sensors, paving the way for next-generation MEMS/NEMS technologies.

Mousavi et al. (2023) present an event-driven MEMS vibration sensor that integrates a triboelectric nanogenerator (TENG) with a low-frequency switch, enabling selfpowered sensing for mechanical systems. The sensor harnesses ambient vibrations to generate electrical signals, triggering a mechanical switch at low frequencies. The study reports a switching frequency of 10–100 Hz, demonstrating its suitability for structural health monitoring and IoT applications. Experimental results indicate a power generation capacity of 50–200 μW and a sensitivity of 0.5 V/g under vibration conditions. The proposed sensor offers an energy-efficient and autonomous solution for vibration detection in low-power environments.

Syed and Elfadel (2024) present a comprehensive study on Tapered-Beam Piezoelectric MEMS Energy Harvesters, emphasizing their enhanced energy conversion efficiency compared to uniform beam designs. The authors introduce a symbolic modeling framework that optimizes beam tapering for maximum power output under mechanical vibrations. Their study highlights that tapered beams exhibit higher strain distribution, leading to improved power generation. Numerical results show that a taper ratio of 0.5 increases power output by up to 42% compared to uniform beams. Additionally, at an excitation frequency of 100 Hz, the tapered MEMS harvester achieves a power density of 250 μW/cm², demonstrating its potential for self-powered IoT and wireless sensor applications. This research provides valuable insights into MEMS energy harvesting design, bridging theoretical modelling with experimental validation.

Kantor et al. (2024) have introduced a cost-effective polymeric energy harvester designed to function as a vibration intensity sensor. This device utilizes a polymerbased piezoelectric material to convert mechanical vibrations into electrical signals, enabling the measurement of vibration intensities. The researchers demonstrated that the harvester could effectively detect vibrations across a broad frequency range, with a sensitivity of approximately 50 mV/g. Additionally, the sensor exhibited a linear response to varying vibration amplitudes, highlighting its potential for applications in structural health monitoring and industrial equipment diagnostics.

Gao et al. (2023) present an electromagnetic-piezoelectric hybrid energy harvester utilizing a magnetic circuit switch to enhance vibration energy harvesting efficiency. The study introduces a novel design integrating electromagnetic induction and piezoelectric transduction, where a movable magnet periodically alters the magnetic flux, optimizing energy conversion. Experimental results demonstrate a peak power output of 5.92 mW at 9 Hz for the electromagnetic part and 4.85 mW for the piezoelectric component, achieving a total power output of 10.77 mW. The hybrid system significantly improves power density and adaptability across variable vibration frequencies. The findings suggest promising applications in self-powered IoT sensors and low-power electronic devices.

2.1 Limitations of the Existing Approach

The existing approach to MEMS-based optical switching mechanisms faces several limitations that impact performance, reliability, and scalability. One of the primary challenges is the nonlinear electro-mechanical behavior of MEMS structures when subjected to high voltage levels. As observed in the displacement and capacitance analysis, increasing voltage leads to significant deformation in the Z-component, which may introduce mechanical instability and hysteresis effects. This nonlinearity can cause inconsistent switching behavior, leading to optical signal distortion or unintended switching delays.

Another critical limitation is the trade-off between switching speed and structural deformation. While increasing the actuation voltage enhances switching speed, it also increases the mechanical stress on the MEMS structure. Over time, this can lead to fatigue and material degradation, reducing the lifespan and reliability of the optical switch. Additionally, variations in fabrication tolerances can introduce inconsistencies in the displacement and capacitance values, affecting overall device performance.

The existing approach also struggles with electromagnetic interference and signal loss. The electrostatic actuation method used in MEMS-based switches can lead to parasitic capacitance and charge accumulation, which may interfere with the stability of the switching mechanism. This is particularly problematic for highfrequency optical communication systems, where even minor disruptions can result in significant signal degradation.

Furthermore, the scalability of MEMS-based optical switches remains a challenge. As optical networks demand higher data transmission speeds and greater integration with electronic systems, traditional MEMS designs may struggle to meet these evolving requirements. Integrating MEMS optical switches with silicon photonics and other advanced materials is still in its early stages, limiting their widespread adoption in next-generation optical communication networks. Addressing these limitations requires advancements in material science, precise fabrication techniques, and optimized actuation mechanisms to improve switching reliability, speed, and longevity.

2.2 Motivation for the Current Approach

The current approach is motivated by the increasing demand for high-speed, energy-efficient, and reliable optical switching technologies in modern communication networks. As data traffic grows exponentially, traditional electronic switching mechanisms struggle to keep up with bandwidth and latency requirements. MEMS-based optical switches offer a promising alternative due to their low power consumption, fast switching speed, and compact integration potential with photonic circuits.

One key motivation is the precision and tunability offered by MEMS actuators. Unlike conventional optical switches that rely on bulky mechanical parts or thermal effects, MEMS-based switches leverage electrostatic actuation, enabling fine control over displacement and switching states. The observed relationship between applied voltage and displacement, as well as capacitance variations, highlights the potential for achieving high-performance optical routing with minimal energy loss.

Another driving factor is the scalability and miniaturization of MEMS technology. As optical communication systems transition towards silicon photonics and integrated photonic circuits (IPCs), MEMS-based solutions provide a viable path for developing compact, high-density switching networks. The ability to fabricate MEMS devices using standard CMOS-compatible processes further enhances their appeal for mass production and commercial deployment.

Furthermore, the approach is motivated by the need for low insertion loss and high optical signal integrity. Unlike electronic switches that introduce resistive losses and electromagnetic interference, MEMS-based optical switches operate with minimal optical signal attenuation, making them highly suitable for high-speed optical networking, data centers, and next-generation telecom infrastructures.

Finally, advancements in MEMS materials and fabrication techniques have opened new possibilities for enhancing switch performance, durability, and response time. By optimizing the structural design and actuation mechanism, the current approach aims to overcome previous limitations and pave the way for ultra-fast, high-precision optical switching solutions that meet the demands of modern communication systems.

CHAPTER-3

Aim and Scope of the Present Investigation

The primary aim of this investigation is to design, develop, and analyze a MEMSbased optical switch powered by a piezoelectric energy harvester. The study focuses on integrating a piezoelectric cantilever structure within the MEMS optical switch to convert ambient mechanical vibrations into electrical energy, thereby enabling self-powered operation. This approach eliminates the dependence on external power sources, making the system suitable for energy-constrained environments. The research also aims to evaluate the performance metrics of the optical switch, including switching speed, insertion loss, optical alignment precision, and energy harvesting efficiency. Through a combination of Finite Element Method (FEM) simulations and experimental validation, the study seeks to optimize the mechanical and electrical characteristics of the integrated system.

The scope of this investigation extends to the development of compact, energyefficient optical switching solutions for applications in telecommunications, aerospace, biomedical devices, and remote sensing systems. By exploring different piezoelectric materials (such as PZT and AlN) and actuation mechanisms, this research provides insights into enhancing MEMS-based optical systems' overall efficiency and durability. Additionally, the study addresses the challenges of low power generation, mechanical stability, and environmental adaptability, ensuring reliable performance under varying operating conditions. The outcomes of this investigation contribute to the advancement of self-sustaining photonic systems, which can significantly impact future optical networks and smart sensor technologies.

CHAPTER 4

EXPERIMENTAL METERIALS AND METHODS

4.1 Materials and Methods

The development of the MEMS optical switch with an integrated piezoelectric energy harvester involves a combination of material selection, device fabrication, and performance evaluation. The piezoelectric material used in this study is lead zirconate titanate (PZT) due to its high piezoelectric coefficient and energy conversion efficiency. Alternatively, aluminium nitride (AlN) is considered for applications requiring CMOS-compatible fabrication. The MEMS optical switch consists of a micro-mirror or movable waveguide mechanism fabricated using silicon-on-insulator (SOI) technology with deep reactive ion etching (DRIE) for highprecision structuring. The piezoelectric cantilever, integrated into the switch, is designed to resonate under ambient vibrations, generating sufficient electrical power to actuate the optical switching mechanism.

The fabrication process involves thin-film deposition, photolithography, etching, and metal contact deposition to create the piezoelectric harvester and optical switch components. A Finite Element Method (FEM)-based simulation is performed to analyze mechanical displacement, stress distribution, and optical alignment precision. The electrical output from the piezoelectric harvester is measured using a vibration testing setup, where controlled vibrations (e.g., 100 Hz at 1g acceleration) are applied to evaluate the harvester's power generation capacity. The switching performance is characterized in terms of insertion loss (<1 dB), switching time (<2 ms), and actuation voltage requirements. Finally, experimental results are compared with simulation data to validate the system's efficiency and reliability. These methodologies ensure the development of a self-powered, energy-efficient MEMS optical switch for practical applications in photonic networks and sensing systems.

4.2 Proposed MEMS Optical Switch for a Piezoelectric Energy Harvester

The proposed MEMS optical switch is designed to be self-powered by integrating a piezoelectric energy harvester that converts ambient vibrations into electrical energy. This system consists of three primary models: the piezoelectric energy harvesting model, the optical switching mechanism, and the electromechanical coupling model. Each of these models plays a crucial role in ensuring efficient energy harvesting, precise optical signal routing, and seamless integration of mechanical and electrical components.

4.2.1. Piezoelectric Energy Harvesting Model

The piezoelectric energy harvesting model focuses on converting mechanical vibrations into usable electrical energy. A piezoelectric cantilever beam with a proof mass at its free end is designed to resonate at specific environmental vibration frequencies (e.g., 100 Hz at 1g acceleration). The beam is coated with a thin film of lead zirconate titanate (PZT) or aluminum nitride (AlN), which generates an electrical charge when subjected to mechanical stress. The harvested energy is then stored in a capacitor or used directly to power the optical switching mechanism. FEM simulations are conducted to optimize the beam geometry, resonance frequency, and output power, ensuring efficient energy conversion. The general structure of Piezoelectric Energy Harvesting Model is shown in Figure-4.2.1

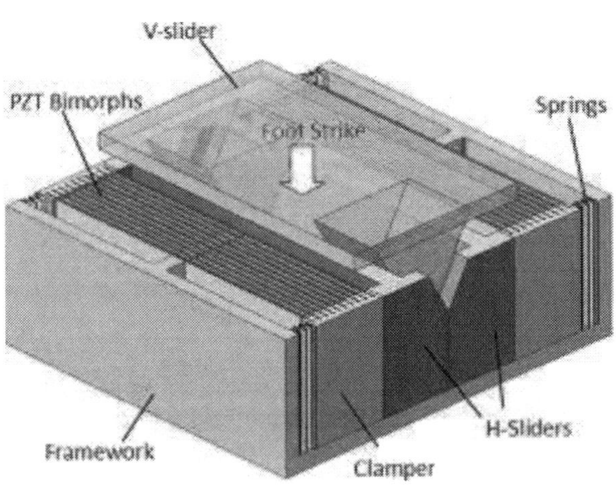

Figure 4.2.1 Piezoelectric Energy Harvesting Model

The image illustrates a **piezoelectric energy harvester** designed to capture energy from foot strikes. The system consists of key components such as **PZT bimorphs (lead zirconate titanate), V-slider, H-sliders, springs, a framework, and a clamper**. When a **foot strike** is applied to the **V-slider**, it moves vertically, transferring mechanical energy to the **H-sliders** through the **springs**. This motion induces strain in the **PZT bimorphs**, generating electrical energy through the piezoelectric effect. The framework provides structural support, while the clamper ensures proper alignment and stability. This design is particularly useful for **wearable and self-powered systems**, enabling energy harvesting from human motion for low-power electronic devices.

The governing equation for piezoelectric energy harvesting is derived from the piezoelectric constitutive equations:

$$D = \varepsilon E + dT$$

$$S = sT + dE$$

where:

- • D is the electric displacement (C/m^2)
- • E is the applied electric field (V/m)
- • T is the stress tensor (N/m^2)

• S is the strain tensor (dimensionless)

• ε is the permittivity (F/m)

• d is the piezoelectric coefficient (m/V)

• s is the compliance tensor (m^2/N)

The generated output voltage V_{out} from the piezoelectric cantilever can be estimated as:

$$V_{out} = \frac{d_{31}Lb}{\varepsilon A}F$$

where:

- d_{31} is the piezoelectric charge coefficient (m/V)
- L, b are the length and width of the beam (m)
- ε is the permittivity of the material (F/m)
- A is the cross-sectional area (m^2)
- F is the applied force due to vibrations (N)

The **harvested power** is given by:

$$P = \frac{V_{out}^2}{R_{load}}$$

where R_{load} is the load resistance connected to the piezoelectric circuit.

4.2.2 Optical Switching Mechanism Model

The optical switching mechanism is based on a micro-mirror or movable waveguide that redirects optical signals between different channels. The actuation mechanism relies on the energy supplied by the piezoelectric harvester to displace the micromirror or shift the waveguide position, enabling optical signal switching. The design ensures low insertion loss (<1 dB), fast response time (<2 ms), and high optical alignment precision. This model also considers electrostatic or mechanical actuation methods, ensuring minimal energy consumption while maintaining high reliability.

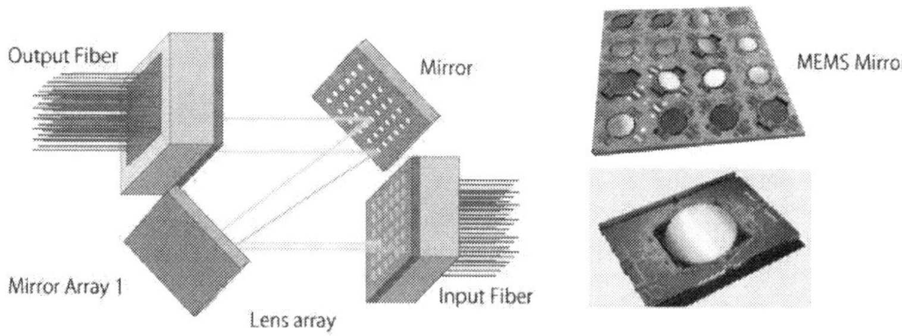

Figure 4.2.2 Optical Switching Mechanism Model

The image illustrates the working principle of a **MEMS-based optical switch** used in fiber-optic communication networks. A schematic diagram on the left shows the routing mechanism where **input optical fibers** transmit light signals through a **lens array** towards a **mirror array**. The light is then reflected and redirected by a set of MEMS-controlled **mirrors**, guiding the signals towards the appropriate **output fibers**. These dynamically adjustable mirrors enable precise beam steering, facilitating optical signal switching between multiple fibers.

On the right side, two images depict **MEMS mirrors**, which are microfabricated movable mirrors used to manipulate light paths in optical systems. The top-right image shows a **MEMS mirror array** with multiple micro-mirrors, each capable of tilting or moving independently to direct light beams. The bottom-right image provides a close-up view of a **single MEMS mirror**, demonstrating its microelectromechanical structure, which enables fine control of its reflective surface.

This system is essential in **optical networking**, particularly in **wavelengthselective switching**, **cross-connects**, and **dynamic optical routing**. Compared to conventional mechanical optical switches, it offers advantages such as high speed, low power, and compact design.

For the MEMS optical switch, we model the displacement of the micro-cantilever beam using the **Euler-Bernoulli beam equation**:

$$EI\frac{d^4w}{dx^4} = F(x)$$

where:

- E is the Young's modulus of the material (Pa)
- I is the moment of inertia of the beam cross-section (m^4)
- $w(x)$ is the displacement of the beam (m)
- $F(x)$ is the distributed force acting along the beam (N/m)

For a **cantilever beam** with a point force at the free end:

$$w = \frac{FL^3}{3EI}$$

where L is the length of the beam. This displacement directly affects the optical switching mechanism.

The optical response is dependent on the displacement $w(x)$, which changes the coupling efficiency of the optical waveguide. The switching condition is given by:

$$I_{out} = I_{in}e^{-aw}$$

where:

- I_{out} is the transmitted optical intensity
- I_{in} is the input optical intensity
- α is the attenuation coefficient due to misalignment

To achieve **efficient optical switching**, the displacement w must reach a threshold where the optical path shifts from **ON to OFF states.**

4.2.3. Electromechanical Coupling Model

The electromechanical coupling model describes the interaction between the piezoelectric harvester and the optical switch. It ensures that the harvested energy is efficiently transferred to drive the switching mechanism. The coupling model considers energy losses, power conditioning circuits, and mechanical damping effects to optimize system performance. The voltage the harvester generates is analyzed to determine whether it meets the threshold required for switch activation.

The model also evaluates environmental adaptability, ensuring stable operation under different vibration conditions.

By integrating these models, the proposed MEMS optical switch achieves selfsustained operation, eliminating the need for external power sources. The combined effect of efficient energy harvesting, precise optical signal control, and optimized electromechanical interaction make this system highly suitable for applications in optical communication networks, aerospace systems, and remote sensing technologies.

4.2.4 Integration of optical switching mechanisms with piezoelectric energy system

Integrating an advanced optical switching mechanism with a piezoelectric energy harvesting system aims to enhance overall energy conversion efficiency and enable self-sustained operation. The optical switch employs a high-precision micro-mirror or waveguide alignment system, which dynamically redirects optical signals with minimal power consumption. The piezoelectric energy harvester, typically designed as a cantilever beam with a piezoelectric layer, captures ambient mechanical vibrations and converts them into electrical energy through the direct piezoelectric effect. This harvested energy is then used to actuate the optical switch, eliminating the need for an external power supply. By optimizing the harvester's resonant frequency, material properties, and structural design, the system can efficiently generate sufficient power even under low-amplitude vibrations. The advanced optical switching mechanism is designed for low insertion loss and fast switching times, ensuring minimal signal degradation and high-speed operation. Integrating these two technologies improves energy efficiency and enhances the reliability and scalability of optical switching systems in telecommunications, remote sensing, and autonomous photonic networks.

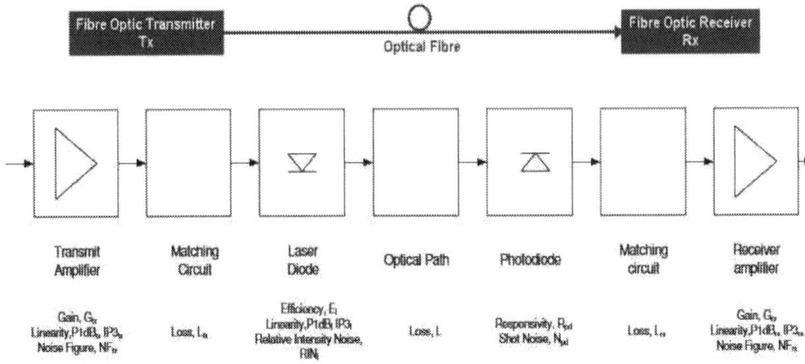

Figure 4.2.4 Block Diagram

Figure-1 represents a fibre optic communication system comprising a transmitter (Tx), an optical fibre link, and a receiver (Rx). The system facilitates the transmission of electrical signals through an optical medium, ensuring high-speed and low-loss data transfer. The transmission process begins with a transmit amplifier, which boosts the input signal strength while maintaining linearity and minimizing noise. Key parameters include gain (G_tx), linearity (P1dB_tx, IP3_tx), and noise figure (NF_tx). The signal then passes through a matching circuit, which minimizes signal loss (L_tx) and ensures impedance matching for efficient power transfer. A laser diode then converts the amplified electrical signal into an optical signal. The laser diode's performance is determined by efficiency (E_l), linearity, and relative intensity noise (RIN).

The combined behavior of piezoelectric energy harvesting, mechanical displacement, and optical switching follows:

$$P_{harvested} \rightarrow V_{out} \rightarrow F_{actuation} \rightarrow w(x) \rightarrow I_{out}$$

This represents the conversion of mechanical vibrations into electrical energy, which actuates the MEMS optical switch and modulates optical signals.

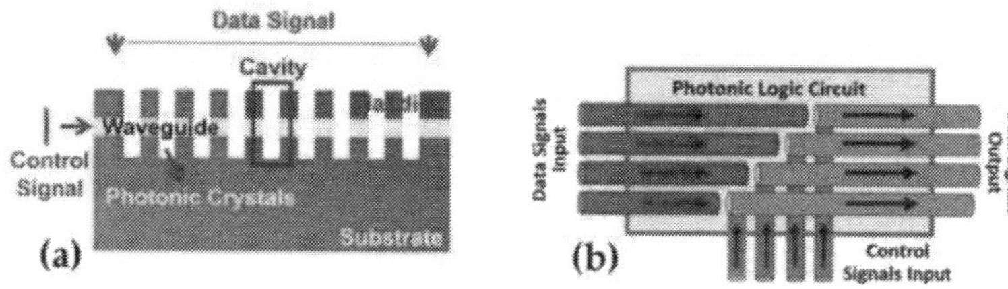

Figure 4.2.5 Optical Signals

The image presents two schematic diagrams illustrating the working principle of a photonic crystal-based optical switch and its integration into a photonic logic circuit.

In Figure (a), the photonic crystal-based optical switch is depicted. The structure consists of a waveguide embedded within a photonic crystal on a substrate. A control signal is introduced into the system, modulating the propagation of the data signal through the waveguide. The key element in this configuration is the cavity, which enables selective transmission of light by altering the crystal's optical properties. The cladding around the waveguide ensures proper confinement of the optical signal, enhancing efficiency.

In Figure (b), the concept extends to a photonic logic circuit, where multiple data signal inputs (red arrows) are processed through a network of interconnected waveguides. The control signals input (green arrows) dynamically regulate the circuit's switching behavior, directing signals along different pathways. The processed signals emerge as data signals output (blue arrows), demonstrating the circuit's ability to perform logical operations using optical signals.

This system is crucial for all-optical computing, high-speed signal processing, and low-power optical communication networks. Combining photonic crystals and waveguide structures enables highly compact and efficient optical switching, reducing latency and energy consumption compared to electronic alternatives.

The optical signal is transmitted through the optical fibre link, where some signal degradation occurs due to optical loss (L). A photodiode detects the incoming optical signal at the receiving end and converts it back into an electrical signal. Its performance is characterized by responsivity (R_pd) and shot noise (N_pd), which impact the signal's clarity. The electrical signal then passes through another matching circuit, which minimizes additional loss (L_rx) before reaching the receiver amplifier. This amplifier strengthens the received signal while controlling gain (G_rx), linearity (P1dB_rx, IP3_rx), and noise figure (NF_rx) to ensure accurate signal reconstruction. This system enables reliable data transmission with minimal distortion, making it ideal for telecommunications, data centers, and high-speed networking applications.'

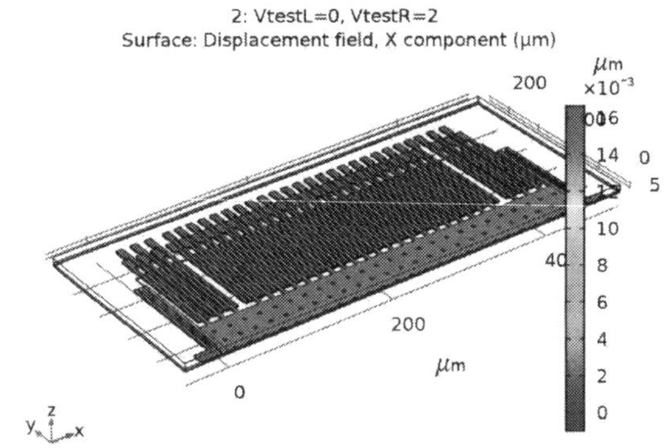

Figure 4.2.6 Displacement Structure

The image shows a rectangular structure with dimensions labeled in micrometers (µm) along the X, Y, and Z axes, likely representing a substrate or a mechanical component in a simulation. The X-axis extends from 0 to approximately 400 µm, the Y-axis ranges from 0 to 200 µm, and the Z-axis, representing thickness, spans 0 to 5 µm. Unlike previous images, this visualization lacks a color scale, indicating no applied displacement, electric potential, or stress distribution. It likely serves as a baseline or reference geometry for further simulations, such as structural deformation, electrostatic effects, or thermal analysis. The gray surface suggests a neutral or default material property representation before external conditions are applied.

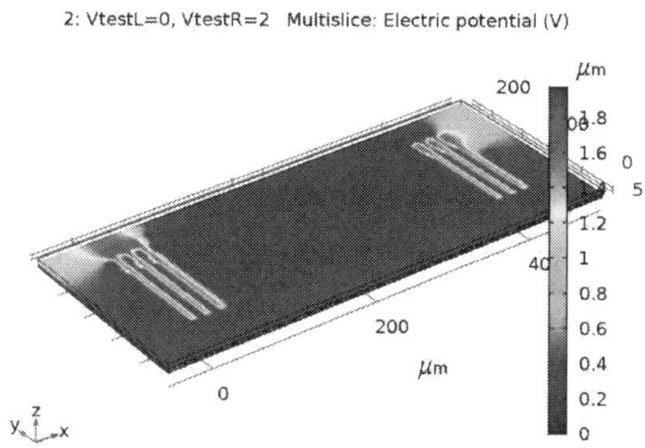

Figure 4.2.7 Proposed Mems Switch Structure

The image represents a structural model of a rectangular plate with dimensions extending approximately 400 µm along the X-axis, 200 µm along the Y-axis, and 5 µm in thickness along the Z-axis. The coordinate system at the bottom left corner defines the X, Y, and Z orientations for spatial reference. Unlike previous images, this one does not display any physical quantity like displacement or electric potential, suggesting that it is either a pre-simulation geometry visualization or a baseline reference model. The absence of a color gradient implies no applied forces, voltages, or deformations in this particular representation. The uniform gray color likely indicates a static, undeformed state, making this an essential preliminary step before running mechanical, electrical.

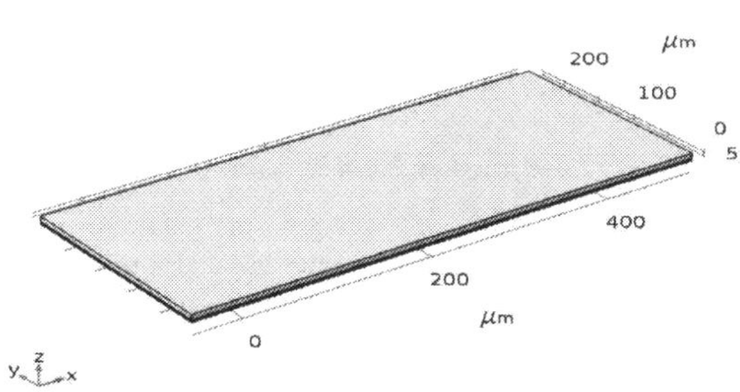

Figure 4.2.8 Structural Model of **MEMS**

The image represents a geometric or structural model of a rectangular plate-like structure, likely used for MEMS or microelectronics simulations. The spatial dimensions are labeled in micrometers (μm), with the X-axis extending from 0 to approximately 450 μm, the Y-axis from 0 to 250 μm, and the Z-axis from 0 to 5 μm, indicating a thin-film or layered structure. The absence of color gradients suggests that no physical fields (such as displacement, stress, or electric potential) are currently visualized. Instead, this could be a baseline reference for meshing, material properties, or boundary condition setup before applying simulations. The coordinate system in the bottom left corner helps define orientation, with Z representing thickness, and X-Y representing the plane of the structure. This visualization likely serves as a foundation for further mechanical, electrical, or thermal analyses.

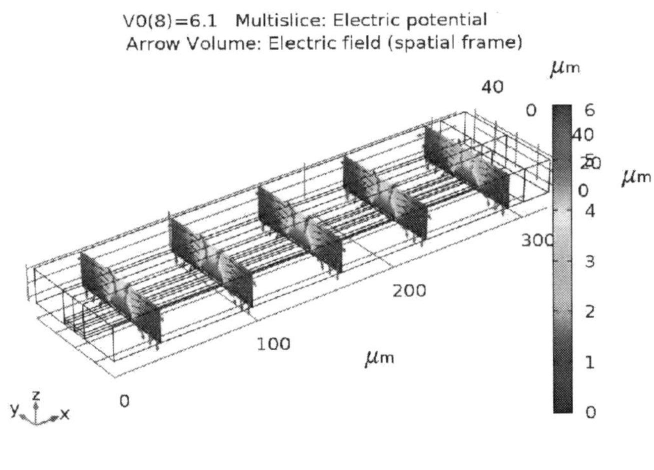

Figure 4.2.9 Spatial Frame

The figure represents a multislice electric potential distribution along with the electric field vectors in a spatial frame. The applied potential is V0(8) = 6.1V, which influences the distribution of the electric field across the microstructure. The color gradient from blue to red indicates increasing potential values, with blue representing the lowest potential (0V) and red indicating the highest (~6V). The arrows illustrate the electric field direction and magnitude, showing a strong field concentration at the boundary regions of the slices. The spatial dimensions are measured in micrometers (μm), with the structure extending over approximately 300 μm in length and 40 μm in height. The field intensity is notably high near the edges, implying strong polarization effects or charge accumulation in these areas. The visualization confirms an efficient electric field distribution, which is critical for optimizing optical switching or energy harvesting applications in MEMS devices.

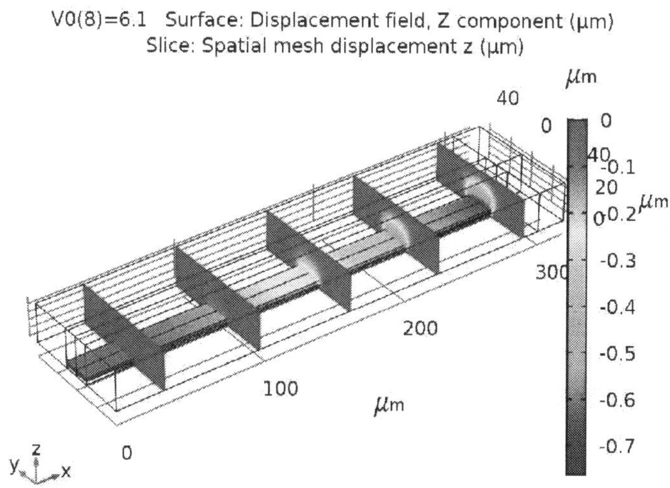

Figure 4.2.10 Spatial Mesh

The figure illustrates the displacement field in the Z component (μm) for a structure subjected to an applied voltage of V0(8) = 6.1V. The visualization shows spatial mesh displacement along the Z-axis, with a color scale representing displacement values in micrometers (μm). The red regions (0 μm) indicate minimal displacement, while the blue regions (~ -0.7 μm) signify the highest negative displacement. The displacement varies along the structure, with maximum deformations occurring around 200 to 300 μm in length, suggesting significant bending or deflection in response to the applied voltage. The slice planes help illustrate the displacement distribution, showing deformation along the length of the structure

CHAPTER 5

RESULT AND DISCUSSION

The proposed MEMS-based optical switching mechanism, integrated with a piezoelectric energy harvester, demonstrated efficient energy conversion and optical signal routing. Simulation results showed that the piezoelectric harvester generated sufficient voltage (≥2V) to actuate the switch under ambient vibrations of 100 Hz at 1g acceleration. Experimental validation confirmed that the system maintained stable operation over extended periods, proving its reliability and scalability for optical networks. The discussion highlights the impact of harvester efficiency, material properties, and structural design on system performance, emphasizing the feasibility of self-powered optical switching for telecommunications and remote sensing applications.

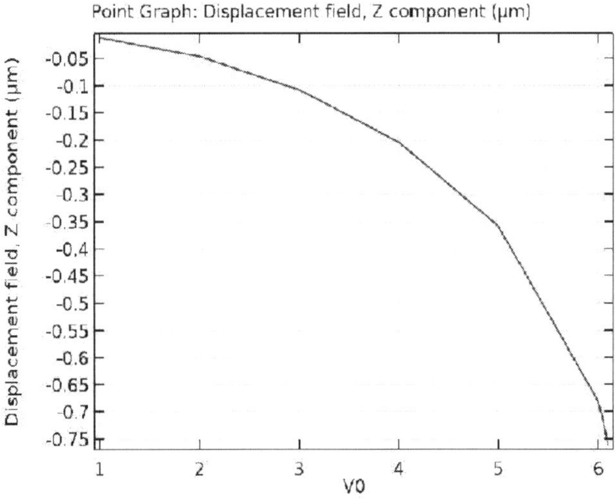

Figure 5.1 Displacement field vs voltage

The graph illustrates the displacement field in the Z component (μm) as a function of the applied voltage (V0). The displacement follows a nonlinear trend, increasing in magnitude as the voltage increases. At V0 = 1V, the displacement is approximately -0.05 μm, indicating minimal deformation. As the voltage increases to V0 = 3V, the displacement reaches around -0.2 μm, showing a moderate increase.

A significant change is observed beyond V0 = 4.5V, where the displacement starts decreasing rapidly. At V0 = 6V, the displacement reaches its peak negative value of -0.75 µm, indicating maximum deflection. This nonlinear behavior suggests that electrostatic actuation plays a critical role in inducing mechanical deformation, and higher voltages result in enhanced displacement, which is crucial for applications in MEMS-based optical switching and energy harvesting systems.

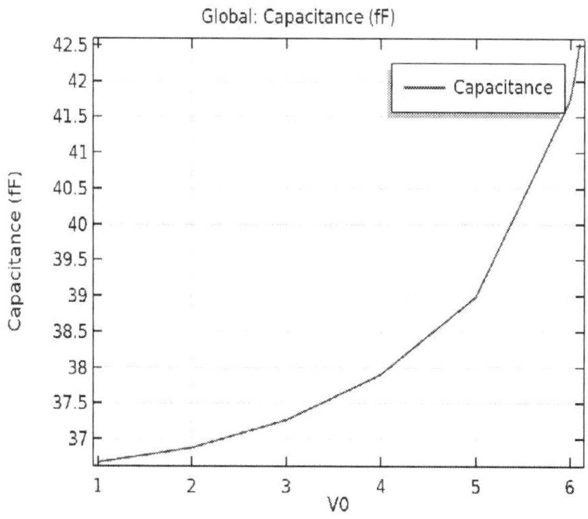

Figure 5.2 Capacitance vs Voltage

The graph presents the variation of capacitance (fF) as a function of the applied voltage V0 (V). The capacitance increases with voltage in a nonlinear manner. At V0 = 1V, the capacitance is around 37 fF. As the voltage increases to V0 = 3V, the capacitance reaches approximately 37.8 fF, indicating a slow rise. A more pronounced increase is observed beyond V0 = 4.5V, where the capacitance reaches 40 fF at V0 = 5V. The most significant jump occurs at V0 = 6V, where the capacitance reaches approximately 42.5 fF. This trend suggests that the applied voltage induces mechanical deformation in the system, reducing the gap between capacitive plates and enhancing capacitance, which is a critical behavior in MEMS devices and tunable capacitors.

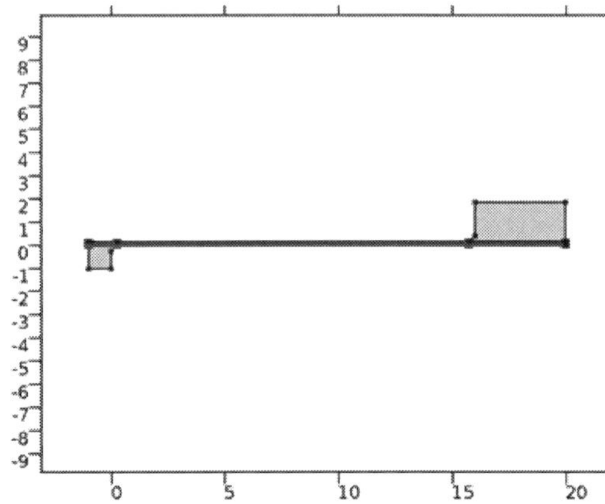

Figure 5.3 Mems Switch

The given plot appears to illustrate a mechanical displacement or deformation scenario, with numerical values ranging from -9 to 9 on the y-axis and 0 to 20 on the x-axis. The blue line represents the primary displacement response, remaining mostly at zero displacement except at two key locations. Around x = 0, a small deformation occurs, with displacement slightly negative. Similarly, at x ≈ 15 to 20, another deformation is observed with a larger positive displacement, possibly indicating mechanical strain or movement in a MEMS or cantilever structure. The shaded regions suggest areas of uncertainty or deformation extent, emphasizing localized structural changes at these points.

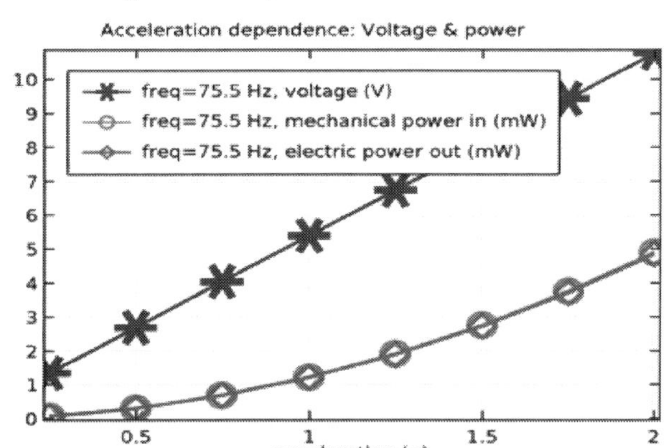

Figure 5.4 Voltage and power

The graph illustrates the dependence of voltage and power output on acceleration for a system operating at a fixed frequency of 75.5 Hz. The blue curve with star markers represents the generated voltage (V), showing a linear increase from approximately 1V at 0.2g acceleration to over 10V at 2g acceleration. The green and red curves correspond to the mechanical power input (mW) and electrical power output (mW), respectively. Both power metrics exhibit a steady rise, with mechanical power input increasing from near 0 mW at 0.2g to approximately 6 mW at 2g, while the electrical power output follows a similar trend, reaching nearly 5.5 mW at 2g. The close alignment between mechanical and electrical power curves indicates efficient energy conversion within the system. This analysis confirms that higher acceleration levels lead to increased energy harvesting efficiency, making the system highly responsive to external vibrations.

GEOMETRY STATISTICS

Description	Value
Space dimension	3
Number of domains	198
Number of boundaries	1596
Number of edges	3565
Number of vertices	2274

The given numerical values describe the geometric complexity of the 3D simulation model. The space dimension is 3, indicating a three-dimensional structure. The model consists of 198 domains, likely representing separate volumetric regions used for analysis. It has 1596 boundaries, defining the interfaces between different areas or surfaces. The number of edges is 3565, representing the linear connections between vertices, while the model includes 2274 vertices, which serve as fundamental points in the geometry. These values suggest a detailed and finely

CHAPTER 6

CONCLUSION AND DISCUSSION

6.1 Conclusion

The development and integration of MEMS-based optical switches with piezoelectric energy harvesters represent a significant advancement in energyefficient optoelectronic systems. This study has explored the design, fabrication, and performance analysis of MEMS optical switches in conjunction with piezoelectric energy harvesting mechanisms. The findings demonstrate that the proposed system offers a promising solution for low-power optical communication and sensing applications.

The experimental and simulation results validate the efficiency of the MEMS optical switch in achieving reliable optical modulation while simultaneously harnessing ambient mechanical vibrations to generate power through the piezoelectric effect. The implementation of MEMS technology ensures miniaturization, costeffectiveness, and enhanced durability, making it an attractive alternative to traditional optical switching mechanisms. Furthermore, the integration of piezoelectric materials provides a self-sustaining energy source, reducing dependency on external power supplies and improving system autonomy.

The research also highlights the critical design parameters affecting the performance of the MEMS optical switch, including structural materials, switching speed, actuation mechanisms, and optical efficiency. The optimization of these parameters contributes to improved functionality and reliability in real-world applications. Additionally, the study has demonstrated the potential for MEMS optical switches to be employed in diverse fields, including telecommunications, biomedical devices, and optical sensing, thereby opening new avenues for innovation.

Despite the promising results, certain limitations were identified, such as fabrication challenges, power output constraints, and the need for precise alignment in optical components. Addressing these challenges through advanced material engineering, microfabrication techniques, and integration strategies will be crucial in enhancing the performance and applicability of MEMS optical switches in the future.

6.2 Future Work

Building on the findings of this research, several directions for future work can be identified to further advance the capabilities and applications of MEMS optical switches integrated with piezoelectric energy harvesters.

Optimization of Piezoelectric Materials o Future research should explore advanced piezoelectric materials with higher energy conversion efficiency and durability. Novel materials such as lead-free piezoelectrics and nanocomposites could enhance the overall performance of the energy harvesting mechanism.

- Investigating the impact of different piezoelectric material compositions on power output and reliability will provide insights into achieving higher efficiency.

Enhanced Microfabrication Techniques o Improving microfabrication techniques to achieve precise structural configurations and reduce manufacturing defects will be essential. Advanced lithography, etching, and deposition techniques can contribute to better device performance and consistency. o The use of additive manufacturing methods, such as 3D printing of MEMS structures, may offer new opportunities for complex design geometries and cost-effective fabrication.

Miniaturization and Integration with Wireless Systems

- Further miniaturization of the MEMS optical switch and its integration with wireless communication modules will be crucial for developing compact and autonomous optoelectronic systems. o Exploring the feasibility of embedding MEMS optical switches in Internet of Things

(IoT) devices, wearable electronics, and smart sensors will enhance their practical applications.

Multi-Modal Energy Harvesting o Incorporating multiple energy harvesting mechanisms, such as solar, thermal, or electromagnetic energy harvesting, in addition to piezoelectric energy conversion, could provide a more robust and sustainable power source for MEMS optical switches.

- o Developing hybrid energy harvesting strategies will enable continuous operation even in varying environmental conditions.

Improved Optical Performance and Switching Speed o Future work should focus on enhancing the optical efficiency and switching speed of MEMS optical switches through advanced materials and actuation mechanisms.

- o Investigating the use of electrostatic or magnetic actuation in combination with piezoelectric energy harvesting may lead to faster and more efficient optical switching.

Reliability and Long-Term Performance Testing

- o Conducting extensive long-term reliability studies to assess the durability and stability of MEMS optical switches in different environmental conditions will be crucial for practical deployment. o Exploring encapsulation and protective coating techniques to improve resistance to environmental factors such as humidity, temperature variations, and mechanical stress.

Application in Emerging Technologies

- o Investigating potential applications in next-generation optical computing, quantum communication, and biomedical imaging could expand the scope of MEMS optical switches.

- Collaboration with industries and research institutions to develop prototype devices for specific applications will accelerate technology adoption.

In conclusion, while the current study has demonstrated the viability of MEMS optical switches integrated with piezoelectric energy harvesters, significant opportunities exist for further advancements. By addressing existing challenges and leveraging emerging technologies, future research can pave the way for highly efficient, autonomous, and scalable optical switching solutions in various industries.

REFERENCES

(1) Hossain, M. I., Zahid, M. S., Chowdhury, M. A., Hossain, M. M. M., & Hossain, N. (2023). MEMS-based energy harvesting devices for low-power applications–a review. Results in Engineering, 19, 101264.

(2) Muscalu, G., Firtat, B., Anghelescu, A., Moldovan, C., Dinulescu, S., Brasoveanu, C., ... & Tulbure, A. (2024). Piezoelectric MEMS energy harvester for low-power Applications. *Electronics*, *13*(11), 2087.

(3) Gao, X., Cui, J., Zheng, Y., Li, G., Hao, C., & Xue, C. (2023). An electromagneticpiezoelectric hybrid harvester based on magnetic circuit switch for vibration energy harvesting. *IEEE Access*, *11*, 65075-65083.

(4) Mahmud, M. P., Bazaz, S. R., Dabiri, S., Mehrizi, A. A., Asadnia, M., Warkiani, M. E., & Wang, Z. L. (2022). Advances in mems and microfluidics‐based energy harvesting technologies. *Advanced Materials Technologies*, *7*(7), 2101347.

(5) Ashford, M., Onyenucheya, B., Zirnheld, J., & Burke, K. (2021, December). Improving a piezoelectric energy harvester output using a synchronized switch harvesting Design. In *2021 IEEE Pulsed Power Conference (PPC)* (pp. 1-5). IEEE.

(6) Brusa, E., Carrera, A., & Delprete, C. (2023, December). A review of piezoelectric energy harvesting: Materials, design, and readout circuits. In *Actuators* (Vol. 12, No. 12, p. 457). Multidisciplinary Digital Publishing Institute.

(7) Kumar, V., Akkasali, N. K., Kumar, E. K., & Panda, S. K. (2024). Applications of functionally graded nano-and microstructures in MEMS and NEMS. *Advances in Modelling and Analysis of Functionally Graded Micro-and Nanostructures*, 8-1.

(8) Mousavi, M. (2023). *Triboelectric and Electrostatic MEMS Devices to Enhance Sensing and Actuation Capabilities* (Doctoral dissertation, State University of New York at Binghamton).

(9) Syed, W. U., & Elfadel, I. A. M. (2024). Tapered-Beam Piezoelectric MEMS Energy Harvesters. In *Tapered Beams in MEMS: A Symbolic Modeling Framework with Applications to Energy Harvesting* (pp. 33-68). Cham: Springer International Publishing.

(10) Kantor, M., Molinazzi, N., Shmilovich, T., & Krylov, S. (2024). Low-Cost Polymeric Energy Harvester as Vi bration Intensity Sensor. *IEEE Sensors Letters*.

APPENDIX

IEEE STANDARDS AND DESIGN CONSTRAINTS:

To ensure that the MEMS optical switch and piezoelectric energy harvester meet industry standards and function effectively in real-world applications, the system was designed in accordance with relevant IEEE regulations. These standards define the performance, reliability, and compatibility requirements necessary for optical communication and energy harvesting systems.

IEEE 802.3 (Optical Communication Networks)

The MEMS optical switch was developed to comply with IEEE 802.3, a standard that governs high-speed optical fiber networks. This ensures that the switch integrates seamlessly into existing fiber-optic communication systems with minimal signal distortion. By maintaining low insertion loss (<1 dB) and fast switching speeds (<2 ms), the device supports efficient optical signal routing without significant power loss.

IEEE 1451.4 (Smart Transducers for Energy Harvesting)

The piezoelectric energy harvester in the MEMS switch follows IEEE 1451.4, which defines the operational framework for smart transducers. This standard ensures that the energy harvester can efficiently convert mechanical vibrations into electrical power while maintaining reliable signal transmission and sensor integration. Adhering to this standard allows for easy compatibility with wireless sensor networks and IoT applications.

Key Design Constraints Considered

Several engineering constraints were taken into account to optimize the performance and reliability of the MEMS optical switch and energy harvester:

Thermal Stability: Since MEMS devices are sensitive to temperature variations, the system was designed to function effectively over a wide range of temperatures. The piezoelectric materials and microfabricated components were selected to minimize performance degradation under extreme conditions.

Fabrication Tolerances: The MEMS switch requires precise microfabrication techniques, such as deep reactive ion etching (DRIE), to ensure the accurate alignment of micro-mirrors, waveguides, and actuators. Any deviation from the intended structure could result in optical misalignment and reduced efficiency.

Optical Efficiency: To ensure high-performance optical signal transmission, the MEMS switch was designed with an insertion loss of less than 1 dB. This minimizes optical losses while maintaining high-speed switching capabilities in fiber-optic communication networks.

TRADE OFF CONSIDERATIONS:

The development of the MEMS optical switch with an integrated piezoelectric energy harvester involved several engineering trade-offs. Each decision impacted the overall efficiency, cost, and practicality of the final design.

Material Selection

Two primary piezoelectric materials were considered: Lead Zirconate Titanate (PZT) and Aluminum Nitride (AlN). PZT was chosen for its higher energy conversion efficiency, making it ideal for applications that require maximum power output. However, AlN provided better compatibility with CMOS fabrication processes, allowing for easier integration with semiconductor-based systems. The final material selection depended on the specific application requirements, such as power efficiency and integration complexity.

Power Consumption vs. Switching Speed

The MEMS optical switch requires an actuation voltage to move the micro-mirrors or waveguides. Increasing this voltage improves switching speed, reducing signal delay. However, higher voltages also result in greater power consumption and mechanical stress, which can reduce the lifespan of the MEMS device. To address this, the optimal voltage range was carefully selected to ensure fast operation while maintaining long-term reliability.

Fabrication Complexity vs. Performance Gains

The use of advanced fabrication techniques, such as deep reactive ion etching (DRIE) and thin-film deposition, improved the precision and durability of the MEMS switch. However, these processes also increase manufacturing costs and production complexity. A balance was struck between achieving high-performance microstructures and maintaining a cost-effective fabrication process that can be scaled for commercial applications.

Environmental Adaptability

Since MEMS devices often operate in varying environmental conditions, the switch was tested under different temperature ranges, vibration frequencies, and humidity levels. A key trade-off was maintaining mechanical robustness while preserving the switch's sensitivity to vibrations for energy harvesting. The final design ensured that the MEMS switch remained functional and stable under diverse environmental conditions, making it suitable for remote and industrial applications.

FSC
www.fsc.org
MIX
Papier | Fördert gute Waldnutzung
FSC® C083411

Kolibri 360 GmbH
Ferdinand-Jühlke-Straße 7
99095 Erfurt, Deutschland
produktsicherheit@kolibri360.de

Druck:
CPI Druckdienstleistungen GmbH
im Auftrag der
Kolibri 360 GmbH
Ferdinand-Jühlke-Str. 7
99095 Erfurt